Koji

(A Japanese Orphan Boy)

By Jooji Matsumoto

Kagami Projects   POB 4187 Albuquerque ,NM   87196

Koji

(A Japanese Orphan Boy)

By Jooji Matsumoto

Illustrations by Dan Noyes

Editing by Karen Klett

Ichikawa

Deru kugi wa utareru..........The *nail* that sticks out gets hammered down.
Japanese saying

I was born in 1951. My mother named me Jooji.[1] My mother was Japanese[2] and my father was an American GI. She was unmarried and unable to care for me so she took me to the local orphanage in Ichikawa. I was born in Chiba prefecture-the area right next to Tokyo. Ichikawa was a town of around 4000 people. It was near the mountains. It was quiet. It was a rural village where people lived on small family plots.

---

[1] Jooji means' farmer' in Japanese.

[2] I never met either of my birth parents and only know my mother's name from my birth certificate.

People's homes were simple. They were made of wood with thatched roofs. Or if they had more money-their home would have a wood roof. Bamboo and pine trees grew in their yards. In the forest on the edge of our neighborhood were more trees and bamboo. The forest was our playground away from the orphanage.

The families in Ichikawa grew rice and vegetables. Some raised chickens. Some worked a trade like carpentry or made clothes. Few people commuted. There were no vehicles in my neighborhood. People rode bicycles and walked. Some neighbors had horses. Every home had a picture of the Japanese Emperor[3] on their wall.

---

[3] Emperor Hirohito –who reigned from 1926 until his death in 1989. Traditionally the Emperor was considered Divine and he was a temporal ruler as well as a spiritual one. In 1946 his Divine status changed although he was still revered in a unique way in Japan.

The orphanage where I lived was very simple. The floor was dirt and the roof was thatched. [4]Life was communal at the orphanage. There were around 15 kids living there with the staff. There was no running water at the orphanage-they brought water in for drinking and cooking. There was an outhouse. We spoke an informal or slang Japanese. We all ate in the same room. Rice and vegetables were our daily diet. Food was donated but there was not a lot of food and some days the portions were small. There was one rag that hung on the wall to blow your nose. A man with a metal probe came to the orphanage once a month and cleaned our ears with it. We all slept in the one room at night-the kids and the staff.

We went to the communal bath house in the village to bathe. [5]That bath house had a divider between men and women. I was curious as to

---

[4] The thatched roof house pictured here was the common country home in Japan during this era and had been for centuries.

[5]Segregated communal bath houses are still common in Japan.

what the woman's side looked like so I peeked under the divider. The men laughed uproariously at that. Soon I felt embarrassed by what I had done.

I was an unusual child. I was curious about the world as all children are but I would ask more questions and explore. I was not afraid in Ichikawa. I would walk around the village and meet people. Other children preferred to stay at the orphanage. I made friends easily which is not the typical Japanese way. In Japan all aspects of life are carefully planned including friendships. I and two other friends from the orphanage would walk to the forest and we would play there. The forest was an escape from the village. Mieko looked after us. She taught me about which kids to avoid and which were nice. She also taught me about which wild plants were edible. I would hang out with her and her brother. We ate mushrooms and shoots to snack on. And we played with beetles![6]

---

[6] Bug pets are a popular and elaborate hobby in present day Japan.

We caught Rhino beetles and had them pull carts made out of leaves or eggplant scraps. It was really fun. When I was a kid they seemed huge and were like pets for us. They were quite strong and could pull the eggplant carts. It was fun to spend hours in the forest playing with the beetles. The creek in Ichikawa, near our orphanage, was clear and smelled fresh. We loved to play in it during the summer heat and loved the cool soft water.

The water in the village of Ichikawa attracted birds like the cuckoo, starlings, ducks, and geese. Occasionally we would see a large bird like a duck or crane.

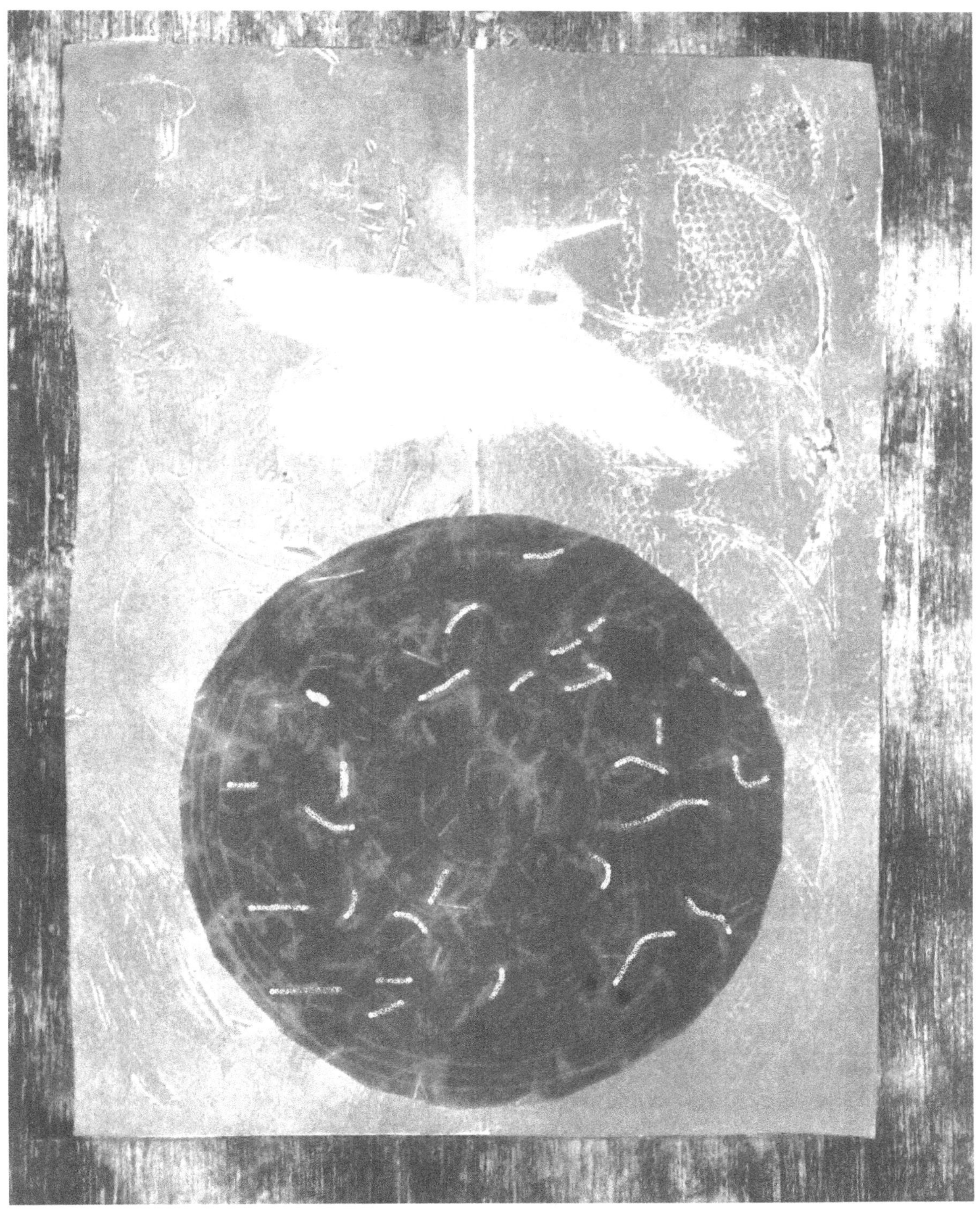

I remember talking with the villagers. The men would talk more about their lives, their work occupations and sometimes would remind me that I was like them and that I would grow up and get old like them age and lose hair.

One lady showed me how she planted rice. [7]She started the rice in little pans in her house. Then they would transplant them in the fields right behind their house. The homes were simple but there was always a place in the home for worship or contemplation. Tea bushes were everywhere. And everyone's homes had tea. Powdered tea, tea mixed with rice, plain tea, tea for celebrations, tea for illness- there were many variations. [8]We would put the tea leaves in our mouths for a snack.

Conversations always came back to the values of Japanese society-duty and honor and preserving the family name and reputation. As orphans we were a little different-our family name carried less weight-and I suppose it made us a little freer than the average Japanese kid. Duty and honor and honesty were evident in all aspects of life. To not try your best was simply not done.

---

[7] Rice is the basic staple of the Japanese and the Asian diet. Rice cultivation in northern Asia is difficult so wheat products are substituted for rice.

[8] Tea is a staple of the Japanese diet. The tea ceremony elevates drinking tea to a contemplative and restorative practice. Drinking tea in Asia can have relaxing and curative associations.

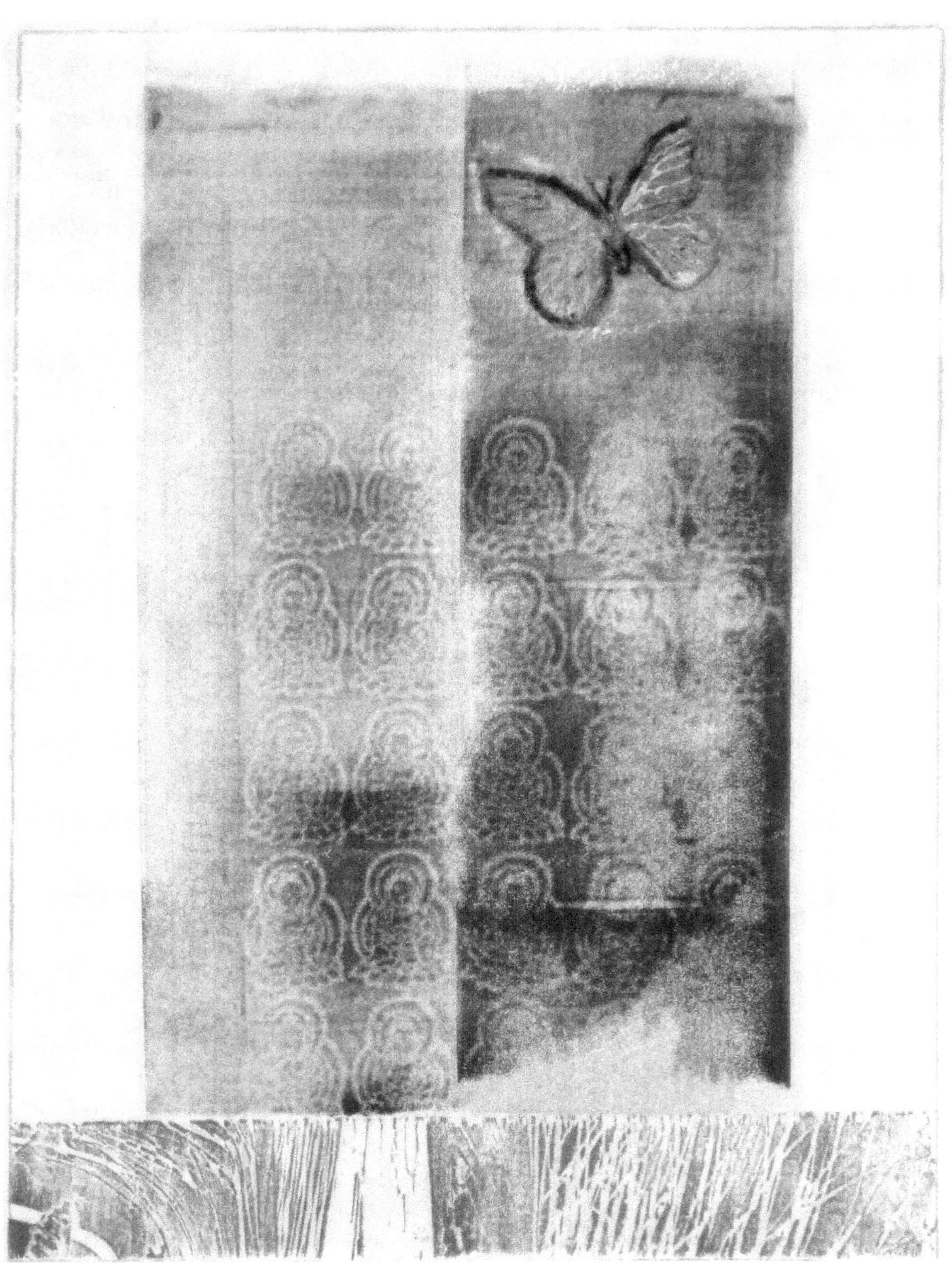

Shinto shrines were everywhere in the village. [9] And incense stands were in front of them. People would go out and light incense and pray at the shrines. I would often go through the village and smell incense burning at a shrine and see nobody around. I like the idea that we are from the world and are part of it and need to live in harmony and equality with all life. Shinto festivals were very interesting to watch. People prayed, they sang, they drank sake, they carried floats. It was a real celebration of lots of people in the neighborhood. Fireworks were set off too .During the festival I heard flute music being played in homes and in the streets. And people-mainly men-would play the drums.

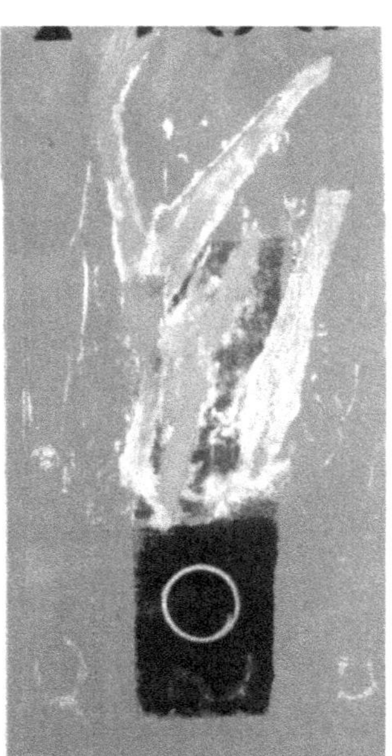

---

[9] Shinto is an animistic religion that has numerous gods of heaven and earth. In the Shinto worldview all life is charged with kami-divine spirits-that inhabit all matter. Shinto is a liturgical religion with a priestly class and accompanying temples and rituals.

Sakura, Cherry blossom trees, are very important in Japan. When they bud out the whole town gets interested and excited. I learned the tree was very important-it was beautiful, sturdy and could live a long time. The tree was a symbol of Japan. For Shinto followers it was especially important as Kami- divine spirits- lived in the tree and made it holy. We were told that many of the trees were planted in the United States Capitol emulating the Sakura trees of Japan. There were other trees too - the maple with bright red leaves in Autumn and pine trees that were green in every season.

Some of the villagers were hesitant to talk to me and the other orphanage kids. Sometimes people would come to the orphanage with donations and they would look at me differently and that made me feel funny. I and most kids in the orphanage were the result of a relationship between a Japanese woman and a foreign man-usually a armed forces soldier stationed in Japan. Some people did not like us for several reasons-we were not pure Japanese and we were a reminder of the occupation. But some people in the village-particularly the mothers of my friends-thought we were fine. They let me into their homes to play with their children.

At the orphanage I was a difficult kid. I asked more questions. I complained more. They would tell me to hush up and I would not be quiet. One time they made me wear shoes that were too small. They hurt my feet and I told them so. They told me to wear them anyway. To let them know I was serious-I put poop in the shoes and that solved that problem! They let me wear my other shoes after that. Or I would go barefoot.

Japanese society has a number of holidays and festivals-New Year, Spring Festival, Harvest Moon festival, Children's festival. The orphanage did not celebrate any of them. Our birthdays were not celebrated either. Many of the kids in the orphanage were not friendly to each other and there was tension in the orphanage. The orphanage staff did their best for us but there was not enough food and clothing to go around.

When I was six I had went to the home of an American couple that had three blonde children-all older than me-and I had stayed for a weekend. The blonde family of five had many many rules. Rule 1- I had to wear my shoes the whole time. Rule 2- I had to hold the cutlery a certain way during meals. (It was the first time I held cutlery as I was used to eating with chopsticks.)Rule 3- keep my elbows off the table. There were many rules about eating and I ended up breaking them all. By the time I left the next day I had broken around 18 house rules. And I never got used to the fact that in their home the toilet was located right next to the bathtub. (In Japan-the toilet is always in a separate room.) After I broke the 18th rule I was relieved to go back to the orphanage.

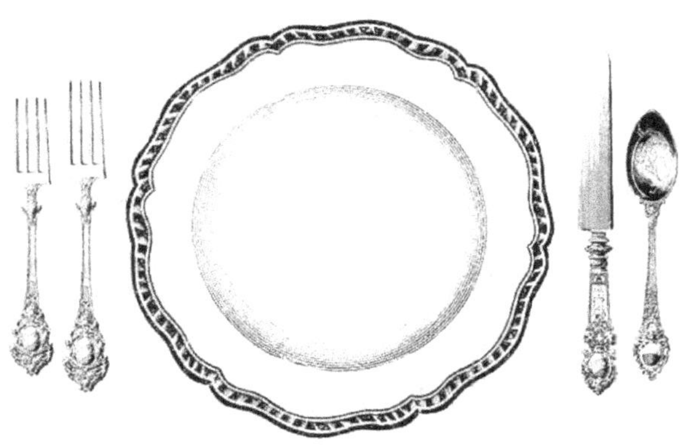

I lived in the Ichikawa orphanage for another 4 years.

Matsudo

I was moved to a new orphanage in Matsudo when I was around 10.[10]
Matsudo was a suburb of Tokyo that was urban. The streets were paved
and lined with shops, businesses, and family homes. People traveled by
bicycle and car and bus. Many people had gardens and some grew
vegetables but it was not the quiet rural village of Ichikawa where I first
grew up.

All of us at the orphanage went to the local school and learned with the
other village children. I enjoyed learning and my teachers and schoolmates.
Science and math were my favorite subjects .Many of my classmates were
mixed ancestry and had a Japanese mom and an American dad. Many were
bilingual-they talked Japanese with mom and English with both parents. I
learned a little English during this time. There were also children of Air
Force soldiers there-generally all Anglo. We tended to think they were
spoiled kids. They were loud, they liked to attract attention to themselves
and some seemed selfish and egotistical. They were just normal American
kids but, they were odd kids, to us-raised in the Japanese way.[11]

One day I was introduced to an American couple who were interested in
me visiting their home with some other orphanage boys. I went to their
house with 2 other boys from the orphanage. I was 12 years old. The other
boys were scared of these white people in their home with a nice flower
garden. I liked the house and I liked the couple. I was comfortable. And I

---

[10] Matsudo is one of 100 places in Japan noted for spectacular Cherry Blossom displays along the Edo
River.

[11] The book 'The Chrysanthemum and the Sword' explores the Japanese society that I grew up in that
stressed Duty, Honor and Emperor.

knew the toilet would be located next to the bath and it did not bother me as much as the other boys. Soon after the visit the orphanage lady asked me if I would like them to be my parents. I said yes and so did another girl at the orphanage. Soon after they told us to pack our things and move to their home.If it went well-we would be adopted. My parents adopted me and a girl from the orphanage that I grew up with.

I was adopted for several reasons. I was curious about the world beyond the orphanage. And that included the home of the couple who adopted me. I did not look pure Japanese and this was also attractive to my parents . We left the orphanage in a big taxi.

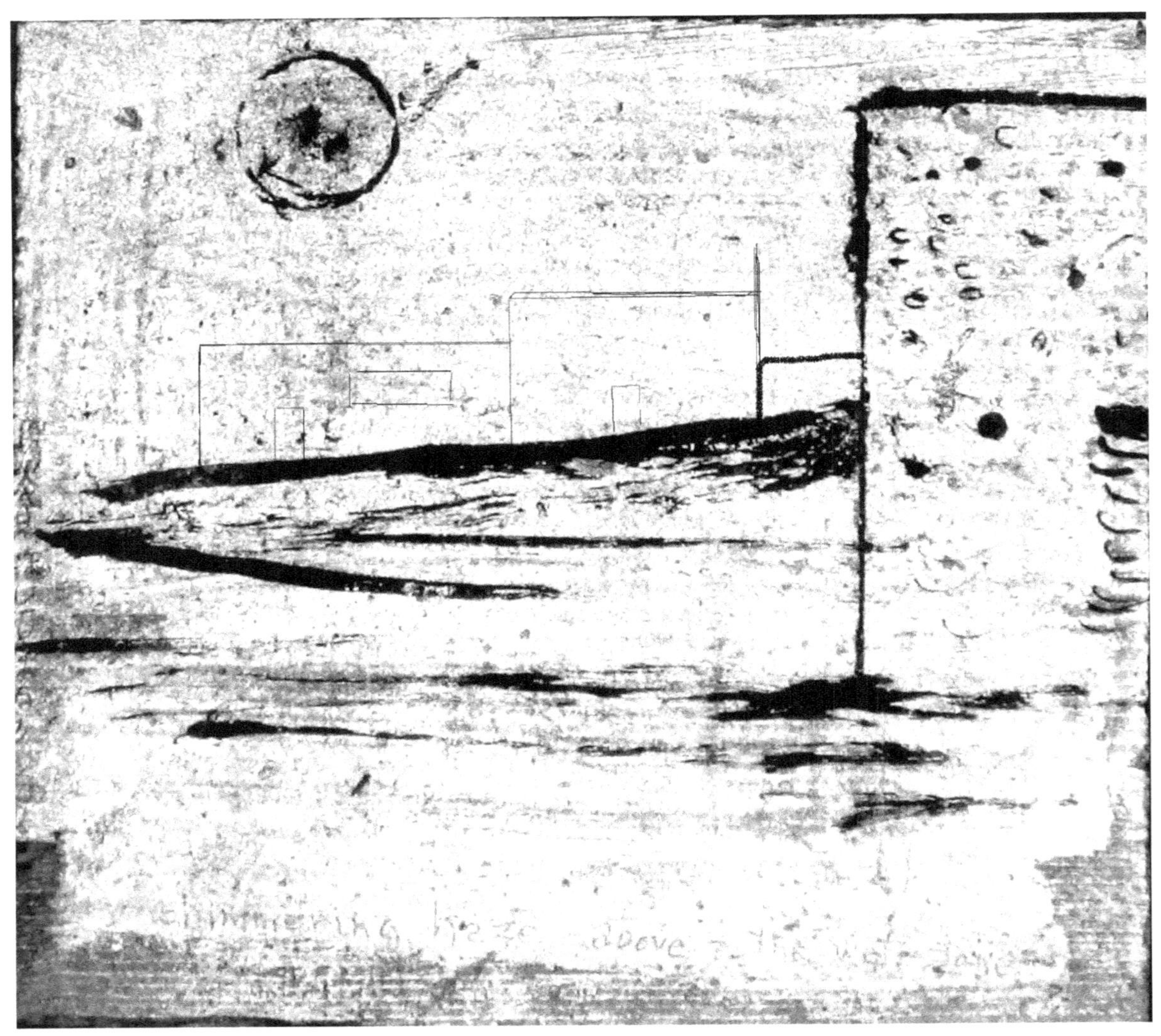

Matsudo was urban. There were cars and concrete. In fact it was the first time I saw a taxi cab and it scared me-a great big car with lights on. . My dad was working for the US Government. He did testing of US GI's –to get them ready for college. Mom worked as a legal secretary. My parents rented a three story house near Matsudo-a town of 2000 people. It was the home of a rich surgeon .It was filled with art-vases, hanging scrolls, wood prints and screens- and a picture of the Emperor hung on the wall. There was a nice garden with a pond that had koi fish. I had my own room. We had a gardener and a maid.[12] In my room I had a chest. I began to collect and read books in English. I collected pamphlets and booklets about Japan, about culture and history. I kept them all in a cabinet in my room. It was a way I learned about Japanese art, about making things with a sense of dedication and making things that were simple yet elegant.

In our new home our cultural education began. We attended school and we learned proper Japanese language and writing and took lessons in folk dancing. They also took us to museums and temples and gardens. I carefully studied the woodblock prints my parents had and studied how the prints were made by examining how the ink was layered on the prints. I could see what colors were put on and in what order. It interested me. And my family celebrated the festivals in Japan along with our birthdays. And we went to see the cherry blossoms on the trees by the Edo River when the blossoms bloomed. It was with Mom and Dad that I experienced the richness of Japanese art, theater, music and dancing. We went to concerts. Here, in a variety of mediums, were people expressing themselves through making pictures, singing songs, playing instruments and performing in plays.

---

[12] The maid and the gardener offered me unique insights into how they and other Japanese viewed the Occupation Government. The maid thought General Douglas McArthur, the Administrator of Japan, was very wise especially since he granted more civil rights to women and children. The gardener was not so sure of the wisdom of McArthur but accepted him as a decent and sensitive ruler.

In a society like Japan that values group harmony, expression is limited to certain types of expression. In the arts the adults resembled children-they laughed, they sang, they were spontaneous. This was very attractive to me and inspired me to ask for art lessons. In the art lessons and in making pictures I enjoyed the process of mixing ink and the feeling of expression that came from painting the pictures. And I enjoyed the feeling of accomplishment when the lesson was done. The lessons were done in our home where I studied with a Japanese artist. I liked him and I liked painting pictures with the bamboo brush and rice paper. Japanese art stresses intuition and a sense of ordinary beauty. It was liberating for me to finally find a way to be creative. [13]

---

[13] Later in life I would get a degree in Art and I would find myself studying with a Japanese master who worked in porcelain.

Life with Mom and Dad was very different. They gave me a new name- George. There was enough to eat. This was sometimes a problem. I did not like the taste of beef. At dinner I would discreetly put pieces of beef in my napkin and throw it in the trash. I had my own room. My sister had her own room. We lived in a nice house. But it was a big adjustment to go from communal living to living in a home with a mother and father. It took a while for all of us to get to know each other. Mom had very good instincts about how to raise us. She was very patient with my sister and I. Dad was impatient and often perplexed at how we behaved. It took him many years to understand that his quiet Japanese children were not going to become 'instant' noisy American kids that liked baseball, bb guns and hot dogs. After I was adopted I returned to the orphanage to visit my friends. My dad blew up. He did not want me to have friendships with them.

I enjoyed playing with Ko ma-a Japanese top. I loved to fly kites. I enjoyed making origami paper sculptures in my room.

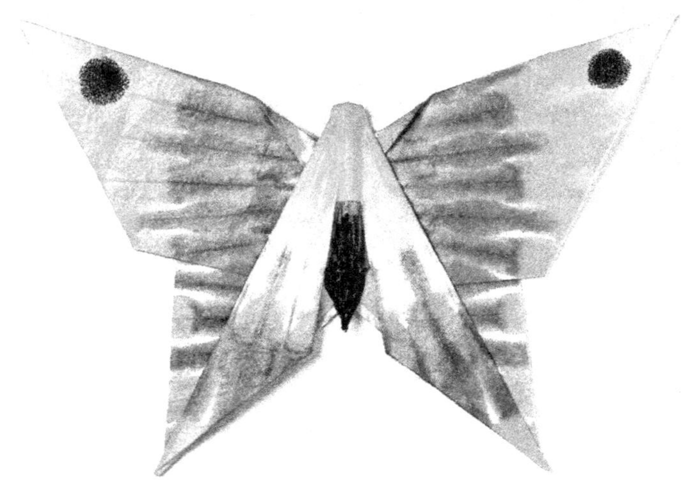

I also had a bamboo cage where I kept my pet bugs. I carefully looked in the yard and found coackroaches, cicadas and rhino beetles in the yard and put them in my bug cage. Many Japanese children did this. I would keep the bugs for a few weeks and then let them go.

In Matsudo I met a friend- Shoji. His dad was a teacher at the high school and raised carp in ponds in his yard. I learned about how to raise carp. I enjoyed visiting my friend and his family and seeing the carp swimming in the ponds. People bought the carp from him for their ponds in their yards. His dad built a pond for my parents and sold them carp. We would help his dad with the carp and the ponds. His dad would read us poems by Basho and other Japanese poets.

Attitudes

Everyone felt bad about World War 2. The Japanese people I talked with felt that the Nazi's had duped the Japanese government and the Japanese people and pulled them into a mess. The war resulted in millions of casualties and the bombing of Japan. Then the American occupation happened. People liked Douglas Macarthur. They thought he and his team rebuilt Tokyo in a good way. There was widespread respect for him. The maids at my parents' house appreciated the fact that Macarthur's Laws forced Japanese law to give Japanese women more civil rights. And they gave children more civil rights too.

In Ichikawa some of the older men in the village wore strange boots. I asked them about the boots. The men wearing the boots were fathers of sons who died in the war. These men were too old to serve and their sons served instead. They wore the dress boots of their sons who died in battle. The boots were one of those sad reminders of the war. The war caused everyone to make sacrifices-rationing food as well as the dangers of military service. Many of the villagers thought the war was insane and foolish but people did not often talk about the war in a disparaging way. The Atomic bombing of Nagasaki and Hiroshima was considered a terrible event. But the terrible atrocities of the Japanese military were never discussed. I learned about them much later in life.

Yet there were lingering ideas in many neighbors that Japanese were superior to other Asians. Japanese were smarter, more hardworking, and more resourceful. Etc.. The idea was –pure Japanese ancestry-not mixed- was superior somehow. This bothered me for several reasons.

The idea that I and my mixed race friends were inferior bothered me. Also I looked at kids who were 'pure Japanese' and wondered why they were not smarter than me. Often in school-mixed race kids had the best grades in class. And when I got older I questioned how more brains could be in the Japanese gene-since it was pure Japanese people that got involved in the disastrous war that ended with terrible casualties and defeat and occupation. I eventually concluded that the benefits of the 'pure Japanese' gene was complete nonsense. It was an insight I kept to myself.

Tachikawa

My family moved out of the surgeon's house and we moved to Tachikawa-a suburb of Tokyo.

The storyteller came often to the neighborhood. I was 13 years old. I enjoyed hearing his stories very much so when he came to the neighborhood I would stop what I was doing and go hear him. He would talk about girls. It was how we learned about girls-how they talked, what they thought about, their desires and their hopes. Girls were a mystery in Japan. Talking to them directly was not encouraged. Talking to them in the presence of their family was fine. Like everything else in Japanese society there were many rules for dating.

Travels in Japan

In Tokyo when we rode the subway the attendants would push people in to make more room so more people could get on the subway car. The attendants would apologize as they did this. My friends and I would ride the trains to different places. I had an allowance. Some of my friends had an allowance or would get money for train tickets from their parents or siblings. One time we went to Kamakura. [14] It would take a couple hours to go to Kamakura. We would enjoy the ride on the train and buy food and talk and look around at the beach. We would look at girls and visit the big Buddha statue. I remember the seafood, the seaweed, and the shrimp. It was all fresh and delicious. My group of friends were mixed race kids also. Hawaiian Americans and Filipino Americans. One full Japanese kid. In other groups we were outsiders but in our group we all had a lot in common. I had a favorite hat I wore-it was a Japanese fighter pilots leather hat.

---

[14] Kamakura is an important destination for Japanese art and culture. It is most known for the massive bronze Buddha statue that faces the Bay of Kamakura.

Duty, Honor and Pachinko was our new motto. The noisy Pachinko palaces where boys and young men stood for hours playing Pachinko machines with flashing lights and steel balls was a mesmerizing pastime.

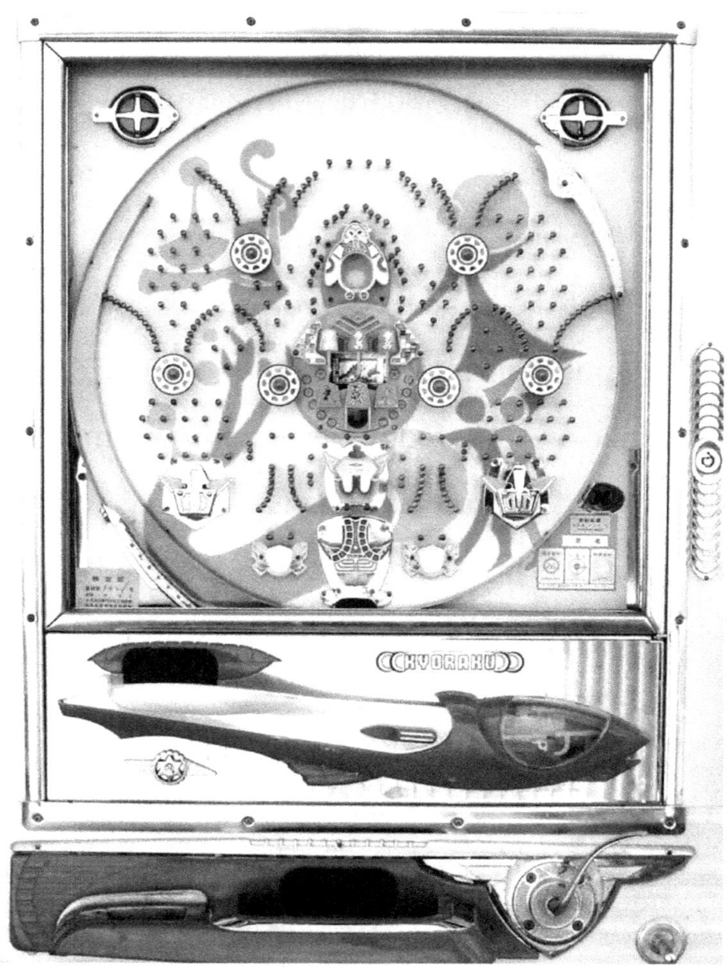

My friends and I went out and traveled around. We took our bikes to the train station and took the train to places. Our bikes were unlocked. I wore my pilot's helmet and a friend of mine did too. On our bikes we acted like we were a motorcycle gang. We would go to Ueno park[15] and enjoyed riding our bikes in the spacious avenues ringed with cherry trees. We walked around, had lunch, and looked at things. We loved exploring around Tokyo. We saw Samurai movies and Godzilla movies.

Ueno Park was a former estate of a Shogun Samurai. It had a museum about natural history. In the museum were exhibits of how people lived in Europe and America. It was fascinating to see how other people lived in other parts of the world.

---

[15] We avoided Ueno park in the Cherry Blossom festival as it was crammed with people. At night it was full of drunken revelers singing songs and laughing. It was a time to let loose and Festivals in Japan are times of Saki, beer, food. laughter and drunken singing.

My friends and I rode our bikes to the Ginza district during the week. The Ginza is a shopping district full of stores, neon signs and restaurants. On weekends the Ginza was packed. Under the neon signs we looked at stores full of cameras, TVs, tape recorders. It was fun to look around. We left our bikes on the bike rack unlocked. We never worried about trouble from thieves.

We were good Japanese boys and misbehaving in public was simply not done. They were a lot of checks and balances to insure you behaved. Your group of pals did not want to attract attention so they would chide you to act right. Worse-a total stranger would stare at you in shame and disbelief. If that did not work -then an authority figure would talk to you and that would be supremely embarrassing to you and to any friends with you. Any action after that-a phone call to your parents or teachers-would qualify as a disaster. [16]We avoided all of that by following the rules. Everyone in Japan followed the rules. All the time. And the rules governed all aspects of life at school, at home, at work, and in public. As a result crime seemed nonexistent. Following the rules takes a toll. But there were ways for people to let go of their stress from work and following the rules of society. Participating in sports, gardening and festivals were ways to relax. Festivals were a time when people let loose and drank and sang and laughed. It was a way to forget about your work, your duties and to let off steam. And the arts were another way for people to let loose -although it was never thought of as 'letting loose'. Art was a way to cultivate your mind.

---

[16] A schoolmate who talked back to the teacher was temporarily banished from his family home. He stayed with his aunt for the night and promptly apologized the next day to the teacher and to his entire class. After the apologizes he was allowed to go back home and live with his Mother and Father.

When I was at the orphanage they did not teach us about Buddhism.[17] In my travels after I left the orphanage I was attracted to Buddhist temples. I had contact with priests and the caretakers who worked there. Their kindness at these quiet places in a bustling noisy city stood out. Their acceptance of me as a mixed race person was a nice and refreshing demonstration of what Buddhism is. (There were sometimes explanations or lectures about the religion which bored me.) The quiet peaceful atmosphere, the smell of incense and the devotion of ordinary people who stopped by to pray and light incense was very nice and I liked it. One message of Buddhism is that the world is just fine as it is. And be grateful you are alive. And all beings are equal both animal and human.

---

[17] Buddhism originated in India and spread throughout Asia. In Japan the main varieties of Buddhism are Pure Land, Zen, Nichirin and Esoteric. All of them value the Buddha, the Sangha (Buddhist Community) and The Dharma (the teaching of Buddha in the 8 fold path that articulates behavior).

Every year I lived there I always knew where Mt Fuji was[18]. It was a landmark and a mountain that had this aura of history and identity about it. For strict Shinto followers it was sacred. And for everyone else it was very important. People gave the mountain respect and they did not articulate ideas about it. And they would go on pilgrimages to the mountain. Those taught me the mountain was very important.

---

[18] Fuji-san is 12,389 feet tall and can be seen for hundreds of miles around it. It figures heavily in Japanese art and culture. See 100 views of Fuji by Hokusai.

There were difficulties and hardships in my childhood. There was some ostracism and hunger in my orphanage years. But there were so many people and experiences that made it great. Many people in the village, in the Buddhist temples and in the towns offered me friendship. I lived the Japanese way- in harmony with others and with nature.

Moving to America

Seiten no heki-reki…...Thunderclap from a clear sky   Japanese saying

After being adopted we began to go to a new school that had mainly American kids in the classes. The kids were all children of Air Force personnel. I grew up with Japanese manners-be humble, don't attract attention to yourself, be quiet, work hard. Above all-do not embarrass yourself with bad behavior. Some of the Air Force kids were just the opposite. They displayed bad behavior. They were not embarrassed to be loud or rude. Some did bad behavior to be funny. And they sneered at each other. This was hard for me to adjust to and comprehend. [19]Yet this was good-they helped prepare me for life in America.

One day when I was 15 Dad announced we were moving to America. We would move into a home like the ones I saw at the museum in Ueno Park.

We moved to Albuquerque when I was 15 years old. I and my sister had a big change to make from Japanese culture to American society

------

[19] Sneering is the worst thing a person can do in a Japanese school. In the American schools it astonished me daily when the kids insulted and sneered at each other. At first I expected the kids to face off after school and fight to defend their honor. Instead they all laughed about it and forgot about the insults.

When we moved to the US. Dad said we did not have room to take my collection of pamphlets and books about Japan. I left them behind. I left my picture of the Emperor behind too.

American society was very different. Getting ahead of others is valued. I was asked over and over by some people' Don't you have any ambition?'[20] I did have ambition but it was understated and that was a problem for some Americans. I did want to succeed but I was not pushy enough for some people. I was amazed when I moved to the US that American society was more selfish than Japanese society. My mother told me this would be different. I was shocked by the variety of goods and merchandise available. The focus on feelings and self expression through clothing, sports, slang, and hobbies seemed overwhelming at times. There were many choices and many seemed frivolous. In Japan- life had been simple.

---

[20] In the Japanese language- one of the forms of the word 'ambition' carries a derogatory meaning. To work hard is normal but to work hard to capture attention and praise at the expense of others is misguided.

The Japanese phrase 'We all eat from the same bowl' summed up much about Japanese values of sharing and community. In America the phrase might be 'My bowl is better than your bowl and I am the only one who eats from it'. It was hard to adjust from the Japanese way to the American way.

After a period of confusion and exploration I learned to like American culture. I like the fact that you can talk about anything here. I liked rock music. Especially Jimi Hendrix. And I got here when the whole counterculture –the Hippies and the youth culture- established itself. Some of the hippy values like harmony and peace were kind of Asian in a way. And I liked the freedom here to study what you want to. I put up a picture of Jimi Hendrix in my room. Jimi Hendrix was my new Emperor.

.

Growing up in Japan was like moving through time and, through epochs of history. Ichikawa was a rural village. Life had not changed there in centuries. Matsudo had elements of rural and modern 20th century life. And Tokyo was a contemporary urban city with mass transit, museums, parks, apartment buildings and sky scrapers. All of it shared Japanese language, a reverence for nature, and values of humility, hard work and cooperation. And although many people looked upon me with suspicion for being half Japanese, many people accepted me as I was and offered me their friendship. As I look back on my life as a Japanese orphan boy-it was a great and unique experience. I don't think you could do it now.

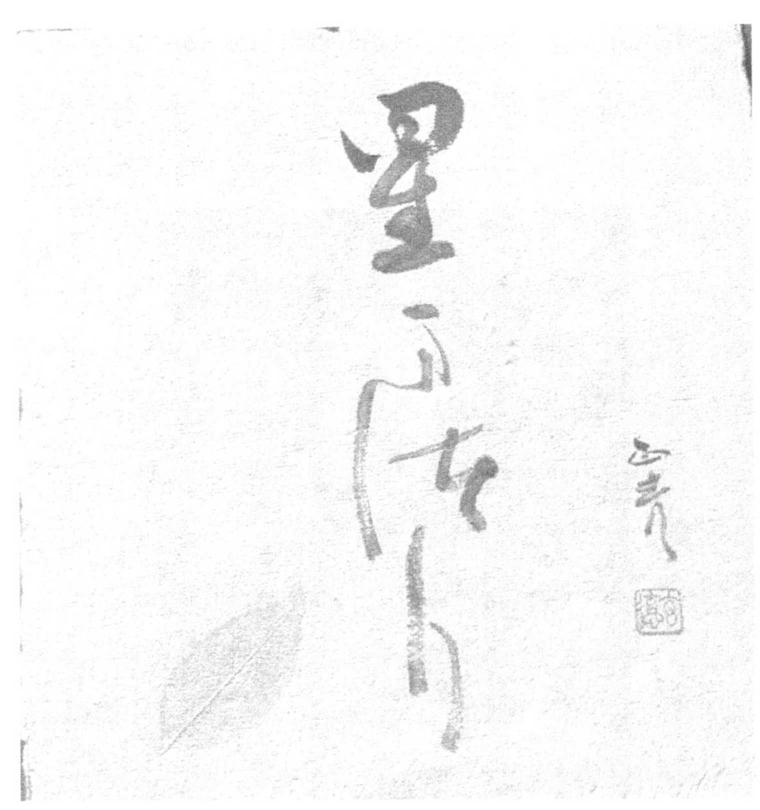

When I was 17 I tried to contact the orphanage and the friends I grew up with. I wrote several letters and received no reply. That was disappointing to me. Sadly, and maybe wisely, we all forgot about orphanage life and moved on. People have asked me if I would like to go back and visit.

I do not wish to return to where I used to live in Japan. My Japan has changed and changed a great deal. The village of Ichikawa is gone. The rice fields and the Ichikawa creek where I watched birds has been paved and has became a city with factories. The people I grew up with have aged-they died, grew up or moved away. They changed and so have I. I accept what happened with wonder and gratitude.

It is impossible to go back in time.

And that is fine.

o   *Fukusui bon ni kaerazu.*   Spilt water will not return to the tray.

Japanese saying

Tori Gate by George Matsumoto

About the Author

George Matsumoto (Jooji) lives in Albuquerque, New Mexico. George has a MA Degree in Art Education. He participated in this book project because his friend Dan Noyes begged him to share his story with others. He makes ceramics and teaches art to children in the summer.

About the Artist

Dan Noyes lives in New Mexico and met George in college 30 years ago. They met in art classes have been friends since. The pictures in this book were inspired by George's life in Japan. Dan's work can be seen at www.dannoyes.net

About the Editor

Karen Klett has degrees in Philosophy and Fine Arts/Theatre. She is the founder of Discover Opera. She is a true Renaissance artist whose work has found expression in acting, poetry, theater and photography. Her photographs can be found at www.ancientcranesong.com